Israel

by Shirley W. Gray

Content Adviser: Professor Sherry L. Field,
Department of Social Science Education, College of Education,
The University of Georgia

Reading Adviser: Dr. Linda D. Labbo,
Department of Reading Education, College of Education,
The University of Georgia

COMPASS POINT BOOKS

Minneapolis, Minnesota

FIRST REPORTS

Compass Point Books
3722 West 50th Street, #115
Minneapolis, MN 55410

Visit Compass Point Books on the Internet at *www.compasspointbooks.com* or e-mail your request
to *custserv@compasspointbooks.com*.

Cover: The Wailing Wall and Dome of the Rock in Jerusalem, Israel

Photographs ©: International Stock/J. G. Edmanson, cover; Bachmann/Photophile, 4; Unicorn Stock
Photos/Remi, 5; XNR Productions, Inc., 6; Jeff Greenberg/Photophile, 7, 15, 20, 24, 25; Horst
Tappe/Archive Photos, 8; Reuters/Jim Hollander/Archive Photos, 9, 13; Reuters/STR/Archive Photos,
10–11, 22; Jean Higgins/Unicorn Stock Photos, 12; Photri-Microstock/Richard T. Nowitz, 14, 26;
Reuters/David Silverman/Archive Photos, 16; Reuters/Rula Halawani/Archive Photos, 18, 40; Inga
Spence/Tom Stack and Associates, 19, 21, 23, 29, 30; TRIP/Dagmar Sizer, 27; Unicorn Stock
Photos/Jeff Greenberg, 28; Warren Lieb/Archive Photos, 31, 34, 38; Photri-Microstock, 32; TRIP/A.
Tovy, 33; Photri-Microstock/Nick Sebastian, 35; TRIP/S. Shapiro, 36–37; Joe McDonald/Visuals
Unlimited, 39; Laurence Argon/Archive Photos, 41; Unicorn Stock Photos/A. Ramey, 42–43;
Norman Owen Tomalin/Bruce Coleman, Inc., 45.

Editors: E. Russell Primm, Emily J. Dolbear, and Deb O. Unferth
Photo Researcher: Svetlana Zhurkina
Photo Selector: Catherine Neitge
Designer: Bradfordesign, Inc.

Library of Congress Cataloging-in-Publication Data
Gray, Shirley W.
   Israel / by Shirley W. Gray.
     p. cm. — (First reports)
   Summary: Introduces the geography, peoples, culture, religious traditions, and history of Israel.
   ISBN 0-7565-0129-6
   1. Israel—Juvenile literature. [1. Israel.] I. Title. II. Series.
   DS118 .G86 2001
   956.94—dc21   2001002745

Table of Contents

Welcome to Israel

"*Shalom*. Peace." This might be the greeting you hear if you visit Israel. Many people who come to this country by air arrive in the city of Tel Aviv.

Israel is in the Middle East on the Mediterranean Sea. On a map, Israel looks like a bridge from Asia to

▲ *Young Israelis*

▲ *The city of Tel Aviv*

Africa. Israel borders the countries of Lebanon, Syria, Jordan, and Egypt.

Israel is a long, narrow country. It is about the size of the state of New Jersey. That's 7,992 square miles (20,700 square kilometers).

You can drive from the north end of Israel to the

▲ *Map of Israel*

south end in one day. In some parts, you can drive from the west side to the east side in less than one hour!

A Homeland

▲ *The remains of a religious building where Jesus taught near the Sea of Galilee in Israel*

The Bible tells many stories about the land of Israel and its people. Jews, Arabs, and other groups of people have lived here for thousands of years.

But Israel is a young country. It was formed in 1948 after World War II (1939–1945). During the war, the German government put many Jews and others into prison camps. Millions were killed. This is now called the **Holocaust**.

▲ *David Ben-Gurion became the first leader of Israel in 1948.*

A story in the Bible tells that God made a promise to Abraham. God said that the land of Israel would belong to the Jews forever. So the Jews call Israel the Promised Land. Many people also call it the Holy Land. Today, Jews from all over the world continue to move to Israel.

▲ Israeli soldiers light candles to remember the Jews who died during World War II.

A gun battle between Israeli soldiers and Palestinians in 2000

Israel now has land that was once called Palestine. The Arabs who live there believe the land is their home. They are called Palestinians. They want to live on the land just as their parents and grandparents

did. The Arabs and Jews continue to fight over who can live on this land.

In Israel, some people speak Hebrew and some speak Arabic. Did you know that the words *camel* and *amen* come from Hebrew?

Living in Modern Israel

In some ways Israel is like the United States. Israeli children enjoy pizza and hamburgers. Companies in Israel make parts for computers. There are many good jobs in Israel.

▲ An Israeli girl enjoys a hamburger.

▲ *An Israeli man holds his daughter while he votes in an election.*

Israel is a **democracy**. People can vote in elections. They must be eighteen or older. The head of government is the prime minister.

Israelis are free to practice whatever religion they want. The three main religions are Judaism, Islam, and Christianity. Religion is important to the people of Israel.

▲ *A Greek Orthodox Church near the Sea of Galilee*

▲ *A bar mitzvah march for a young man at the Western Wall in the Old City of Jerusalem*

The Jewish holidays are official holidays in the country of Israel. The Jewish day of rest is called the **Sabbath**.

▲ An Orthodox Jew prays at the Wailing Wall on the eve of Yom Kippur.

The Sabbath begins at sundown on Friday. It ends at sundown on Saturday. During the Sabbath, many Jewish stores, schools, and businesses are closed.

In the fall, the Jews celebrate the new year on Rosh Hashanah. Children like this holiday. They eat apples dipped in honey. Israelis say this is so they will have a sweet year.

Another Jewish holiday is Yom Kippur. It comes ten days after Rosh Hashanah. Yom Kippur is a quiet day of prayer.

The Jews fast on Yom Kippur. This means they do not eat or drink until after the sun sets. Offices and schools are closed. Even radio and television stations go off the air.

Islam is the religion of Arab Muslims in Israel. The Muslim Sabbath is on Friday. In spring, Muslims celebrate Ramadan.

During Ramadan, which is a sacred time, Muslims

▲ *Palestinian women pray near the Dome of the Rock during Ramadan.*

fast for a month. They eat and drink only after the sun sets. At the end of the month, they have a three-day feast to celebrate.

Family Life

Children in Israel go to school five days a week, as they do in the United States. Families eat lunch together after the children come home from school. Many activities center on the family.

▲ *Israeli schoolchildren get ready to cross a street.*

Israelis grow and eat lots of fruits and vegetables. They also like lamb cooked with spices. A sauce is made from yogurt to go with the lamb.

Some Jewish families do not cook on the Sabbath. They keep a pot of stew in a warm oven and eat it on the Sabbath. This stew is called cholent. It is made from a mix of beef, beans, chickpeas, and potatoes.

▲ A man sells food in the Arab Quarter of Jerusalem.

On Saturdays, families go hiking or have picnics. The picnic basket often has falafel sandwiches inside. They are made with pita bread and fried balls of chickpeas mixed with spices.

▲ *Israelis cook with many kinds of spices.*

Soccer and basketball are popular sports in Israel. Families and friends come to see games and to cheer for their favorite teams. Some basketball teams have players from the United States.

▲ *Israel takes on Hungary in a soccer match.*

A Holy City

▲ *The Dome of the Rock is an important landmark in Jerusalem.*

The capital city of Israel is Jerusalem. Many people say it is a holy city. Christians believe Jesus Christ spent his last days on Earth in Jerusalem. Muslims believe it is where the **prophet** Muhammad was taken into heaven.

▲ *An Ethiopian Jew prays at the Wailing Wall.*

Today Jerusalem has two parts. The Old City is east Jerusalem. The New City extends to the west. Walls and gates divide the Old City from the New City.

Some of the walls are very old. Between 25 B.C. and 13 B.C., Herod the Great built the Temple in Jerusalem. Only one wall of the Temple still stands. It is called the Western Wall or the Wailing Wall.

Jews believe this wall is a holy place. They come to the wall to pray to God. Some visitors write prayers on small pieces of paper. Then they tuck the paper into cracks in the wall.

Palestinian families live outside of the Old City in the Arab Quarter. They have lived there for many generations.

The New City looks like cities in the United States or Canada. It has many new buildings. The streets are busy and full of cars.

▲ *Two businessmen chat in the Arab Quarter of Jerusalem.*

A Dry Land

Thousands of years ago people called Israel the land of milk and honey. The land had food and water for everyone. Modern settlers thought it was dry and bare.

▲ *Scientists study an ancient Roman building in Israel.*

Southern Israel is a desert. It is called the Negev.

In the day, the temperatures often rise to more than 120° Fahrenheit (49° Celsius). Sometimes, less than 1 inch (2.5. centimeters) of rain falls here in a year. In some parts of the United States, that much rain can fall in one hour or less!

◄ *Wild goats called ibex live in the Negev Desert.*

27

North of the Negev is a large lake called the Dead Sea. The water is lower here than anywhere else on Earth. It is about 1,340 feet (408 meters) below sea level.

Most lakes have fresh water. The Dead Sea is filled with salt water. It has so much salt that no plants or fish can live in it.

▲ The Dead Sea is the lowest spot on Earth.

Helping the Land

▲ *Israelis grow watermelon plants under tents near Elat.*

Early Jewish settlers farmed only on the Mediterranean coast. They could not grow enough food for everyone. The government had to buy food from other countries.

Many Jewish settlers still work as farmers. They live on **kibbutzim**. A kibbutz is a farm where everyone lives together and shares the work. Some people cook the meals and some work in the fields. Other

▲ *The Bet Alfa Kibbutz in the Jordan Valley*

▲ *Israeli farmers use drip irrigation.*

people take care of the children. Everyone shares food and money on a kibbutz.

The Jewish people had to find new ways to grow food. They built a huge pipe to bring fresh water to farms in the desert. This is called **irrigation**. Now the farmers grow fruits and vegetables all year in the Negev Desert.

Farmers and scientists worked together. They pumped water out of the Mediterranean Sea. They then took out some of the salt. Then they searched for plants that could live in this water.

One plant they grew is the Negev tomato. Today, Israeli farmers grow so many Negev tomatoes that they sell them to stores in Europe!

▲ *Israeli farmers grow lots of tomatoes.*

▲ *Trees in the Jordan River valley*

The Israeli people planted millions of trees on hills in northern Israel. The roots help hold the soil in place. Now the hillsides do not wash away in the rain.

The Israelis have helped the land. They no longer think their country is dry and bare. They see that it is lush and green. Best of all, they grow enough food for everyone to eat.

▲ *Some Israeli farmers raise trout and salmon on fish farms.*

Living in the Desert

Many Arabs still live in Israel today. One group is called the Bedouins. Their families have lived in the Negev Desert for hundreds of years.

▲ *Bedouins move from place to place with their animals.*

The Bedouins are **shepherds**. They herd goats,
sheep, or camels. They move from place to place
with their herds of animals. The Bedouins live in tents.
They weave cloth for the tents from camel or goat
hair.

A Bedouin shepherd in the Negev Desert

The Bedouins know where to go to find food and water. This is how they can live in this dry, hot land.

The Bedouins are kind people. Often they help others who get lost in the desert. If you visited a Bedouin family, they would serve you their best food.

Plants and animals live in the desert too. They adapt to the harsh land.

The sabra is a cactus that can live without much water. Its fruit has thorns and a thick skin on the outside. The thick skin keeps sweet juice inside. Jewish people born in Israel are sometimes called sabras. This is a nickname.

▲ *The sabra is a cactus.*

▲ *A snake in the Negev Desert*

Snakes and lizards can live in the desert too. They sleep under the rocks and sand during the day when it is hot. At night, the desert cools down. This is when snakes and lizards hunt for food.

Visiting Israel

▲ *Christian pilgrims light candles in Bethlehem.*

For hundreds of years, people have visited Israel from around the world. Many of these people are **pilgrims**. At Christmas, many Christian pilgrims visit the town of Bethlehem. Christians believe Jesus Christ was born there.

Young people from North America or Europe like to come to Israel to work on a kibbutz. Many kibbutzim have small hotels so that tourists can visit.

▲ *Young people from a kibbutz take part in a folk-dancing festival.*

The Old Quarter of Jaffa is now part of Tel Aviv.

The Dead Sea is also a place people like to visit.
It is easy to swim and float in its salty water.
If you visit Israel, you will learn more about the

people who live in this ancient land. You may say
"Shalom" when you come or go. "Shalom. Good-bye.
Thank you for my visit!"

Glossary

democracy—a form of government in which people choose their leaders by voting

Holocaust—the killing of millions of Jews and others by the Nazis during World War II

irrigation—the practice of supplying water to crops through pipes or channels

kibbutzim—small farms in Israel where everyone lives together and shares the work

pilgrims—people who travel to holy places

prophet—a person who claims to speak for God

Sabbath—the Jewish day of rest and worship

shepherds—people who look after sheep or other animals

Did You Know?

- The Hebrew language is written from right to left.

- Israel is known by many names, including Zion and Cana'an.

- The holy book for Jewish people is called the Torah, which means "law." It is also known as the Five Books of Moses.

- Israeli prime minister Golda Meir was raised in Milwaukee, Wisconsin.

At a Glance

Official name: State of Israel

Capital: Jerusalem

Official language: Hebrew (Arabic and English are also spoken)

National song: "Ha'Tikva" ("The Hope")

Area: 7,992 square miles (20,700 square kilometers)

Highest point: Mount Meron, 3,692 feet (1,126 meters)

Lowest point: Dead Sea, –1,340 feet (–408 meters)

Population: 5,842,454 (2000 estimate)

Head of government: Prime minister

Money: Shekel

Important Dates

late 1800s	European Jews begin working to establish a Jewish state in Palestine.
1930s	A large number of Jews and Arabs move to Palestine.
1947	The United Nations divides Palestine into Arab and Jewish areas.
1948	Israel declares itself independent. David Ben-Gurion becomes Israel's first prime minister.
1964	Arab groups form the Palestine Liberation Organization (PLO).
1967	Israel attacks Egypt in the Six-Day War.
1973	Egypt and Syria attack Israel in the Yom Kippur War.
1978	Israel and Egypt sign a peace agreement called the Camp David Accords.
1993	Prime Minister Yitzhak Rabin signs a peace treaty with PLO leader Yasser Arafat.
1995	Yitzhak Rabin is murdered.
2001	Ariel Sharon is elected prime minister.

Want to Know More?

At the Library

Gresko, Marcia S. *A Ticket to Israel*. Minneapolis: Carolrhoda Books, 2000.

Randall, Ronne. *Israel*. Austin, Tex.: Raintree/Steck-Vaughn, 1999.

Thoennes, Kristin. *Israel*. Mankato, Minn.: Bridgestone Books, 1999.

On the Web

CNN Special Reports: Israel at 50

http://www.cnn.com/SPECIALS/1998/israel/

For articles written in 1998 in honor of Israel's fiftieth year

Israel Ministry of Foreign Affairs

http://www.israel.org

For information about the history, geography, and politics of Israel

The Israel Museum, Jerusalem

http://www.imj.org.il/

For an online tour of this remarkable museum

Through the Mail

Israel Nature and National Parks Protection Authority

3 Am VeOlamo Street
Givat Shaul
Jerusalem 95463
Israel
To find out about Israel's parks and reserves

On the Road

The Jewish Museum

1109 Fifth Avenue
New York, NY 10128
212/423-3200
To learn more about Jewish culture around the world

Index

About the Author

Shirley W. Gray received her bachelor's degree in education from the University of Mississippi and her master's degree in technical writing from the University of Arkansas. She teaches writing and works as a scientific writer and editor. Shirley W. Gray lives with her husband and two sons in Little Rock, Arkansas.